WHEN I GROW UP

I'LL BE A CHEF

1 HOUSE SPECIAL

WITHDRAWN

BY CONNIE COLWELL MILLER   ILLUSTRATED BY SILVIA BARONCELLI

AMICUS ILLUSTRATED • RIVERSTREAM

AMICUS ILLUSTRATED is published by Amicus
P.O. Box 1329, Mankato, MN 56002
www.amicuspublishing.us

Paperback edition printed by RiverStream Publishing in arrangement with Amicus.
ISBN 978-1-62243-360-5 (paperback)

LIBRARY OF CONGRESS CATALOGING-IN-PUBLICATION DATA
Miller, Connie Colwell, 1976- author.
I'll be a chef / by Connie Colwell Miller; illustrated by Silvia Baroncelli.
    pages cm. – (When I grow up . . .)
 Summary: "A young boy pretends to be a master chef while cooking in the kitchen
with his dad and shows what it's like to be a professional chef"– Provided by publisher.
 ISBN 978-1-60753-759-5 (library binding) – ISBN 978-1-60753-858-5 (ebook)
 1. Cooking–Vocational guidance–Juvenile literature. 2. Cooks–Juvenile literature.
I. Baroncelli, Silvia, illustrator. II. Title.
 TX652.4.M55 2016
 641.5023–dc23   2015029344

EDITOR   Rebecca Glaser
DESIGNER   Kathleen Petelinsek

Printed in the United States of America at
Corporate Graphics in North Mankato, Minnesota.

HC 10 9 8 7 6 5 4 3 2 1
PB 10 9 8 7 6 5 4 3 2 1

ABOUT THE AUTHOR

Connie Colwell Miller is a writer, reader, and teacher who lives in Mankato, Minnesota. When she was little she always knew she would work with two things: kids and books. Today, her dream has come true. She has written more than 80 books for kids, and she has four wonderful, creative children of her own.

ABOUT THE ILLUSTRATOR

Silvia Baroncelli has loved to draw since she was a child. She collaborates regularly with publishers in drawing and graphic design from her home in Prato, Italy. Her best collaborators are her four nephews, daughters Ginevra and Irene, and organized husband Tommaso. Find out more about her at silviabaroncelli.it

Anna, the server, rushes in. Mrs. Jones has ordered the house special! And guess what? Mrs. Jones is our pickiest customer. I have to make a meal that will knock her socks off!

My staff and I get to work. My sous chef prepares the ingredients I will use for the house special—tortellini. He dices tomatoes. He chops spinach. He minces garlic.

While the noodles boil, I create the sauce. I add the fresh ingredients to a saucepan. I add salt, pepper, and basil too. The pan starts to sizzle.

Now for step two! I mix flour, milk, and cream in a bowl. I slowly add it to the saucepan to make my sauce creamy. I practiced a long time to learn the exact amounts my sauce needs.

The sauce begins to bubble, and the smell is amazing! I taste-test the sauce to make sure all the ingredients are in perfect balance. Today, the sauce needs just a bit more salt.

Now, the noodles are done boiling. The line cook strains the noodles. But I add them to the sauce. I make sure all the noodles are covered in deliciousness!

I scoop some of the tortellini into a wide bowl. I add bread sticks and salad to the tray. I arrange the meal perfectly. Part of a great meal is how it looks.

It's finally ready! Anna brings
the tray to picky Mrs. Jones.

WORDS CHEFS SHOULD KNOW

basil—An herb that is often used in cooking.

house special—The dish that a restaurant is best known for.

line cook—A person who prepares ingredients and helps make meals in a restaurant.

Master chef—A chef who runs the kitchen in a restaurant and has completed the highest level chef training.

mince—To cut into very small pieces.

recipe—A plan that tells chefs how to make a meal.

sous chef—The second chef in the kitchen, whose job it is to help the master chef.

tortellini—A type of noodle that is ring-shaped and has a filling.

Ask an adult to help you with the stove for this recipe. You can be the chef for the night!

WHAT YOU NEED

1 (16 ounce/453 g) package of cheese tortellini
1 (14.5 ounce/411 g) can diced tomatoes
1½ teaspoons (7 mL) dried basil
1 teaspoon (5 mL) minced garlic
¼ cup (65 mL) shredded Parmesan cheese
½ teaspoon (2 mL) salt
¼ teaspoon (1 mL) pepper

WHAT YOU DO

1. Bring a large pot of water to boil. Add the tortellini. Boil the noodles until they are tender, which should be about 10 minutes.
2. While the noodles cook, put the tomatoes in a large saucepan. Add the salt, pepper, basil, and garlic. Stir and cook over medium heat until the mixture begins to bubble.
3. Drain the tortellini. Do not rinse it. Pour the noodles into the saucepan with the sauce. Stir to coat.
4. Serve your tortellini. Sprinkle with shredded Parmesan cheese to make your plates look perfect!